Can you
the eggs?

Jenny Giles
Illustrated by Trevor Ruth

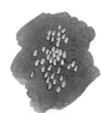

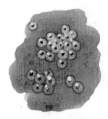

Mother Blackbird
is in the tree.

Her eggs are
in the nest.

Mother Fish
is in the stream.

Her eggs are
in the stones.

Mother Snail
is in the grass.

Her eggs are
under the ground.

Mother Butterfly
is on the flower.

Her eggs are
under the leaf.

Mother Snake
is on the sand.

Her eggs are
in the hole.

11

Mother Frog
is on the leaf.

Her eggs are
in the pond.

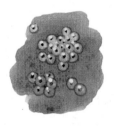

Mother Kiwi
is in the forest.

Her egg is
in the nest ...

15

... under the Father Kiwi.